Girl, Get to Stepping!

Copyright © 2018 by Apostle/Prophetess Ann Har

Girl, Get to Stepping

Published by: The Cheek Consultancy Company
Fayetteville, North Carolina
Cover Design by Chantee Cheek, Your Anointed Designs

Printed in the United States of America

All rights reserved. No part of this publication may be reproduced, distributed, or transmitted in any form or by any means, including photocopying, recording, or other electronic or mechanical methods, without the prior written permission of the publisher, except in the case of brief quotations embodied in critical reviews and certain other noncommercial uses permitted by copyright law. For permission requests, write to the publisher, addressed "Attention: Permissions Coordinator," at the email listed below.

Apostle Ann Ministries
apostleannministries@gmail.com

Publisher's Cataloging-in-Publication data

Harris, Jerry Ann,
     Girl, Get to Stepping: Breaking the religion, tradition, and fear of women in the ministry / Apostle/Prophetess Ann Harris; foreword by Lucinda Moore; Bishop Orrin K. Pullings Sr.
     p. cm.

ISBN-13: 978-0-692-15268-3

1. Women – Christianity —. 2. Religion. 3. Deliverance & Healing Catholic Publishing Company. (2016, July 21). Mary Magdalene: 'First witness to the greatest event in history'. Retrieved from https://www.osv.com/OSVNewsweekly/ByIssue/Article/TabId/735/Art MID/13636/ArticleID/20218/Mary-Magdalene-'First-witness-to-the-greatest-event-in-history'.aspx

pg. 1

Apostle/Prophetess Ann Harris

Scriptures marked AMP are taken from the AMPLIFIED BIBLE (AMP): Scripture taken from
the AMPLIFIED® BIBLE, Copyright © 1954, 1958, 1962, 1964, 1965, 1987 by the Lockman
Foundation Used by Permission. (www.Lockman.org)

Scriptures marked KJV are taken from the KING JAMES VERSION (KJV): KING JAMES VERSION, public domain.

Scriptures marked NKJV are taken from the NEW KING JAMES VERSION (NKJV): Scripture
taken from the NEW KING JAMES VERSION®. Copyright© 1982 by Thomas Nelson, Inc.
Used by permission. All rights reserved.

First Edition

14 13 12 11 10 / 10 9 8 7 6 5 4 3 2 1

Girl, get to Stepping

Apostle/Prophetess Ann Harris

Forward By:
Bishop Orrin K. Pullings Sr., & Stellar Award Winner Lucinda Moore

~ About the Author ~

Apostle/Prophetess Ann Harris is the author of "Winning the War of the Mind." She and her husband, Apostle Neal Harris, are the Founders, Overseers, and Pastors of Daily Walk Ministries Inc. which is located in Fayetteville, NC. Also, they are the Founders and Overseers of "The Walk of Fellowship" churches, both nationally and internationally. They can be viewed weekly the national Christian television on "The Now Network" and on a local television station (CWW 22). Apostle/Prophetess Ann Harris is the founder of "Saved, But Yet Wounded" women's outreach ministry, which is designed to empower women in every aspect. She has *a heart* to see the people delivered and for ministry. She walks in a strong deliverance ministry and flows in the prophetic. Apostle/Prophetess Ann Harris is truly a woman of God after His own heart.

~ Acknowledgment ~

First and foremost, I give all glory and honor to my heavenly Father, His son Jesus Christ, and his precious Holy Spirit for this opportunity, and for inspiring me to write this book. I would like to thank my loving husband, Apostle Neal Harris, and my six children for their support. I want to give acknowledgement to my mother, Minister Annie Campos, for her love and strength. Also, I would like to thank all of the Pastors of the Walk of Fellowship churches, and Daily Walk Ministries for the encouragement and prayers; a special thank you to Minister Christopher Cheek, who is one of my number one supporters.

~Foreword~

In "Girl, Get to Stepping," Apostle Prophetess Ann Harris provides a framework for *women* that will allow them to follow their God-given destiny. While some may be held back by fear, anxiety, and feelings of not being worthy, this book will surly *jolt* the impossible. Using her own life experiences, Apostle Ann ensures that you will move forward with the gifts, talents, and dreams that you have; some realized, and others that you had no idea were inside of you. Get ready to run, because you will be ready to take *flight* once you finish this great book!

-Bishop Orrin K. Pullings Sr.
United Nations Church International of *Richmond, VA*

One word, "Extraordinary!!!" This book is a must read! "Girl, Get to Stepping," will bless your life! Just AMAZING!

-Lucinda Moore, *Stellar Award Winner*
"Walking in My Favor"

Apostle/Prophetess Ann Harris

Table of Contents

- About the Author- pg. 4
- Acknowledge- pg. 5
- Foreword- pg. 6
- Table of Contents- pg. 8
- Prologue- pg. 9
- Introduction- pg. 12
- Chapter 1: Arise and Shine – pg. 16
- Chapter 2: Who is This Power for? – pg. 23
- Chapter 3: Moving Beyond Your Past- pg. 45
- Closing: Girl, Get to Stepping! – pg. 55
- Epilogue- pg. 64
- Prayer- pg. 68
- Questions for You- pg. 70
- Seeking the Lord Scriptures- pg. 72
- Inspirational Scriptures- pg. 76
- Speaking Life and Overcoming Scriptures- pg. 77
- Scriptures for Help- pg. 80
- Personal Notes- pg. 82
- More Information – pg. 87

Prologue

Apostle/Prophetess Ann Harris

Women you have been summoned to, "Get to Stepping!" You have a dream and vision to fulfill. *Arise*, God has need of you; *awaken* oh great army of warrior women for there is a call that awaits you. In order for you to step into the higher calling that God has intended for you, it will require a willing spirit and a deeper level of faith in Him. God has a purpose for you that will require the use of your vision and faith. The alarm has been activated, calling-out to you oh great army of warrior women. Therefore, *arise* to the battlefield and get to stepping because it is *time* to shine.

There is an anointing that has your name on it. You "are" a chosen vessel. God is not looking for someone that is perfect, but for someone that is willing to be washed and sanctified by his Holy Spirit. He is least worried about your past. Congratulations! You have passed the background check! God is awaiting your response to say, "Here I am Lord, send me!"

Both men and women were created in God's image and likeness. God's word does not state anything about its overall intent being only for men or only for women. His word is inclusive, exempting no one, and is unchanging. In other words this means God's word is for *all* men and women. His word has a plan for us all, but are you willing to step into God's plan predestined for you?

Introduction

God may have called some of you into leadership. For example, when He initially called me, He used the character of Moses to instruct me concerning the call upon my life. The revelation he revealed to me was not for the carnal mind to comprehend but was a mystery spiritually discerned. When he called me, I was confused because Moses was a "MAN," and I am a woman. God then told me that he wasn't talking about the natural man, but the anointing that lies on Moses. He correlated the call upon my life with the anointing Moses walked-in just like John the Baptist had the spirit of Elijah (Luke 1:17). This meant that the anointing Moses walked-in would require me to do a lot of fasting, praying, asking, and seeking God. Moses was called to be a Deliverer and also a Prophet which requires fasting, praying, asking, and seeking God. Moses had to go through the wilderness. I also have had multiple wilderness experiences. During the valley, you have to fast, pray, ask, and seek after God because of the price of the anointing. Just as the scripture says that some things only come through prayer and fasting.

[**KJV Matthew 7:7** *"Ask, and it shall be given you; seek, and ye shall find; knock, and it shall be opened unto you."*]

> [**KJV Mark 9: 29** "29 *And he said unto them, This kind can come forth by nothing, but by prayer and fasting."*]

This kind of anointing will allow you to have access to anything because of the "faith" level that is needed in this call. Faith has to increase while in your wilderness because you are not operating on the things you don't see, but only believe.

> [**KJV Hebrews 11:1** *"Now faith is the substance of things hoped for, the evidence of things not seen."*]

Accepting the call as an Apostle, Prophet, and a Pastor was *not* an easy task. At first, I struggled with the fear of what man thought and what man would say about me. One of those fears was dealing with the people's perception of a woman in ministry especially one who preaches. It was difficult battling with this conflict, especially when I knew I was continuing to hear the voice of God in my dreams calling me over and over again. Not only was I hearing the verbal voice of God, but also through dreams and visions while I was sleep and even walking through my house. I eventually began to realize that I allowed fear to hold me hostage and prevent me from stepping into what God has for me. I allowed fear to keep me in its prison; I could feel the weight of how it had me bound. I wanted to shake this yoke lose, so I began to fast, pray, and stay before the Lord to find out who I was and who I would someday become. Soon, open visions started appearing before me and the voice of God began to speak. Shortly after, joy and peace overtook me and I received from God a powerful yoke breaking release. After my release, I mustered-up enough courage to begin stepping-out in faith while trusting God. The more I got to stepping, the more God allowed me to know what Spirit and anointing I would walk in. As I started to go higher in God, He told me that I would need to tell others, "Girl, get to stepping!"

Chapter 1:
Arise and Shine

Girl, Get to Stepping!

Rise to the battlefield warrior women! Surely it would be a shame to discover you are the missing link in your family or in your church because you bowed down and submitted to fear, false teachings, and religious beliefs based on fears. With that being said, this prompts me to discuss an awesome woman of God in the Bible, Mary Magdalene.

Mary Magdalene was a lady that made up her mind that she would get to stepping no matter what! She was not perfect; in fact, Mary Magdalene had many issues. For instance, Jesus had to cast seven demons out of her, but she never allowed this to neither discourage her nor become a setback that would burden her down with shame, but was rather thankful for what Jesus had done. She was thankful for her deliverance, and she expressed her gratitude to Jesus. This was a step of freedom for Mary Magdalene because she began to follow Jesus. During that particular era, women were not allowed to follow Rabbis, which were Jewish teachers of the law; however, Mary Magdalene knew there was a high calling upon her life. The calling upon Mary Magdalene's life was to break the spirit of religion and tradition.

Mary Magdalene was an amazing woman with a powerful testimony to share. She was the first person to testify about the resurrection of Jesus Christ. She was with Jesus during the time of his ministry here on Earth, before the crucifixion, during the crucifixion, after the crucifixion, and was also there to witness his resurrection. After His resurrection, Jesus did not sit around to wait and see if a man would show up or worry about the people's religious beliefs. She was there, in position waiting for Jesus. Jesus knew there was someone on the scene that was qualified for the job… that someone was Mary Magdalene. He had checked-out her resume, and that specific resume made her the *perfect* candidate for the job! Her faithfulness alongside with commitment, humble spirit, and gratefulness towards him were all the qualifications Jesus was looking for. This is why she was chosen for the job to take the first message of the resurrection back to the other disciples. This is the reason why Jesus first appeared to Mary Magdalene after the resurrection according to the scripture Mark 16:9-11, "*9 Now when Jesus was risen early the first day of the week, he appeared first to Mary Magdalene, out of whom he had cast seven devils. 10 And she went and told them that had been with him, as they mourned and wept.11 And they, when they had heard that he was alive, and had been seen of her, believed not."*

The instructions given to Mary Magdalene was: fear not, go quickly, and tell He has risen according to the scripture in Matthew 28: 5-7.

[**KJV Matthew 28:5-7** *"5 And the angel answered and said unto the women, **Fear not** ye: for I know that ye seek Jesus, which was crucified. 6 He is not here: for he is risen, as he said. Come, see the place where the Lord lay. 7 And **go quickly**, and **tell his disciples** that he is risen from the dead; and, behold, he goeth before you into Galilee; there shall ye see him: lo, I have told you."*]

Mary Magdalene knew she had to get to stepping. She couldn't procrastinate, but rather move quickly. She was commissioned to take the gospel to the Apostles; therefore, she was the "first" to preach the good news. The message that she ministered was "He is risen!"

[Fact: On June 10, 2016 Pope Francis, by decree, raised the July 22nd memorial of St. Mary Magdalene to a feast on the church's liturgical calendar. Other than the Virgin Mary, she became the only woman saint assigned a feast and is recognized equal status with most Apostles. The Roman Catholic Church considers her to be "Apostle of the Apostles."]

In order for Mary Magdalene to get to stepping in the way that she did, she had to press beyond any form of fear that could hinder her from accomplishing what she was commissioned to do. God did not give you, me, or anyone else the spirit of fear. If God did not give you fear then who did? God said he gave you the power, love, and a sound mind.

[KJV 2 Timothy 1:7 *"For God hath not given us the spirit of fear; but of power, and of love, and of a sound mind."*]

As a matter of fact, the truth is this: fear is derived from our adversary, Satan. This tactic is designed to keep you paralyzed and scared to step out in faith. Women of God, this is why we must be courageous, step out of religion, and not be bound by fear. God may desire to use you by providing you with a platform on your job, in your church, in your family, or to preach in front of a congregation. Truthfully, it is all about God wanting to receive you; He desires to receive your faithfulness and obedience to Him. Next, let us briefly take a look at Esther; she also responded to the call of God.

[**KJV Esther 4:16** *"Go, gather together all the Jews that are present in Shushan, and fast ye for me, and neither eat nor drink three days, night or day: I also and my maidens will fast likewise; and so will I go in unto the king, which is not according to the law: and if I perish, I perish."*]

Esther is a woman, in the Bible, who *prepared* herself to get to stepping in her calling. When you observe the actions and motives of Esther, you will notice that she focused more on the Jewish race rather than being concerned about herself. Regardless of the traditional beliefs in this time era, Esther prepared herself for her stepping process as you can find stated in this passage of scripture, Esther 4:11, *"All the king's servants, and the people of the king's provinces, do know, that whosoever, whether man or women, shall come unto the king into the inner court, who is not called, there is one law of his to put him to death, except such to whom the king shall hold out the golden, that he may live: but I have not been called to come in unto the king these thirty days."* This passage of scripture shows us that entering into the king's inner court without being summoned can be life-threatening; therefore, Esther could have been put to death but she was determined to get to stepping by faith.

Esther called a fast with no food or drink for three days and nights. Esther denied herself and accepted God's platform for her life because she trusted God. In fact, Esther had not seen the king for thirty days, knew the laws and decrees of the king, and was aware of the risk-taking possibility of ending her own life. Because Esther stepped out in faith and denied herself, she obtained favor from the Lord. As women in the Gospel, we must have faith over fear in order to step into the next dimension in God. So women of God I say to you, "If God be for you, then who can be against you?"

> [**KJV Romans 8:31** *"What shall we then say to these things? If God be for us, who can be against us?"*]

Esther's faith simply says to us, "Girl, get to stepping and let favor shine on the platform God wants to give you."

Chapter 2:
Who is This Power for?

Apostle/Prophetess Ann Harris

There will be a day, to come, that every individual must stand before the Lord. A question that will be asked to you will be, "Whose report did you or did you not believe?" We must seek out the truth so it can keep us free, so the Holy Spirit can lead us, so we can obtain understanding of the Word of God, and to prevent us from being bound by false-doctrines and religious beliefs. Question, "Can women operate under the same power of the Holy Spirit just as men?" So who is this power for?

The apostle Paul spoke about the women whose names are listed in the Book of Life, meaning salvation. This following scripture is what Paul had said about these women in the gospel, Philippians 4:3, *"And I intreat thee also, true yokefellow, help those **women** which with me in the gospel, with Clement also, and with other my fellow labourers, whose names are **in the book of life**."* If all names are written in the Book of Life and we cannot work together here on Earth, then how do we expect to work together in heaven? Both men and women must learn to work harmoniously together *now*, which is why the apostle Paul said "be ye followers of me, even as I also am of Christ" in 1 Corinthians 11:1 (KJV).

Girl, Get to Stepping!

In reality, physically men are stronger than women. For example, there are objects that men can lift and move that women cannot. Women's bodies are not designed to move or lift certain things, but in the spiritual realm that does *not* apply. The bible says in Romans 2:11 that there is no respect of persons with God. Your gifts and callings doesn't recognize gender in the spiritual realm. What if you are the one God called, and was sent to be a deliverer?

Women of God never cut your selves short! Since the beginning of time, the enemy always had something against women. For an example, in the Garden of Eden, the enemy's first attack was to come after the woman to deceive her. However, you must ask yourself, "Why did Satan choose to come after her "first" in the garden?" The answer is this: Satan has an understanding of the power that lies within a woman! I have heard many say things such as: the woman was attacked because Adam was out of place. If Adam was really out of place, why did the enemy choose not to proceed with taking him out first? It was since the beginning of time, our adversary has been persistent with trying to silence and shutdown women. This attacked the women's character in the view of society as the "weaker vessel." If women were really the weakest vessel, do you think the enemy would want to take out the weakest first or the strongest first? The attack in the Garden of Eden was mentioned to show how the enemy first attempted to accomplish this malicious task by manipulation, deception, and lies; Satan also did it by turning the word of God around.

In ministry, I have experienced people approaching my children telling them that God does not use women in the pulpit. My kids were taught the word of God since they were little. When I questioned them about their responses to the people who were telling them that information… they answered "I gave them scripture." I was so amazed at my children's wisdom! In this life, I have come to the realization that you will always have someone challenging your faith and the call of God upon your life. In fact, there is one scripture in particular that people misuse and teach inappropriately which is 1 Corinthians 14:34 *"Let your women keep silence in the churches: for it is not permitted unto them to speak; but they are commanded to be under obedience as also saith the law* (KJV)."

Does the scripture, referenced above, mean women cannot speak? According to scriptures in the Bible, it is clear that women did in fact speak in the temple. In fact, some women prayed and prophesied there just like the prophetess Anna. Anna was a prophetess. A prophet is known as God's messenger. In order for you to release a message from God, first you must be able to speak about God and his message. You can find this scripture stated in Luke 2:36-38, *"[36] And there was one Anna, a prophetess, the daughter of Phanuel, of the tribe of Aser: she was of a great age, and had lived with an husband seven years from her virginity; [37] And she was a widow of about fourscore and four years, which departed not from the temple, but served God with fastings and prayers night and day. [38] And she coming in that instant gave thanks likewise unto the Lord, and spake of him to all them that looked for redemption in Jerusalem."* Anna was close to God, very committed, and had strong spiritual insight. Even in her old age, she proclaimed God's word and served Him with fasting and prayers day and night which you can find quoted above in verse 37 of Luke. She spoke of the Lord to all that looked for redemption. We, as God's people, cannot ignore the facts which are highlighted directly from scripture. If we are not careful, we will become hypocrites just like the Pharisees; the Bible tells us not to be like the hypocrites. This is a testament that God called both men and women, and that women worked in the early church.

Briefly, let us take a look again at the text from 1 Corinthians 14: 34-35, "*³⁴ Let your women keep silence in the churches: for it is not permitted unto them to speak; but they are commanded to be under obedience as also saith the law. ³⁵ And if they will learn anything, let them ask their husbands at home: for it is a shame for women to speak in the church.*" This scripture does NOT imply that women cannot speak in church. I believe this church was in transition. Something new was happening and they did not understand what was taking place. The Bible says my people are destroyed for lack of knowledge (Hosea 4:6) and where there is no vision the people perish (Proverbs 29:18).

The Corinthians had a problem with women being over anything. I believe this particular church experienced women being super excited to be Christians that they did not understand how to use their freedom. Based on scripture, I believe the Corinthian women thought it was an opportunity to confront and question others of their beliefs. Their actions were simply out of order! These women questioned others in public worship, which caused division in the church. It was neither the time nor place to do that during a worship service; these women should have done that at home not in the middle a church service. It is a shame for anyone in church to be out of order because there *is* a time and place for everything! The Corinthian women's mindsets had not yet been renewed. They didn't enhance the scriptures Romans 12:2 and Proverbs 3:13 which that their mind must be renewed, and they must have wisdom and understanding.

> [**KJV Romans 12:2** *"And be not conformed to this world: but be ye transformed by the renewing of your mind, that ye may prove what is that good, and acceptable, and perfect, will of God."*]
>
> [**KJV Proverbs 3:13** *"Happy is the man that findeth wisdom, and the man that getteth understanding."*]

Answer this question for me, "If women were to be completely silent in church, then why do we allow women to sing in choirs, usher, read announcements, and even allow them to orchestrate programs? Okay, here is another question for you, "Would you not be offended if you say "hi" to a lady in church and she does not respond to you? [Would you not consider that rude and would that not cause confusion?] If we want to preach or teach that women must be silent, and if that is what you truly believe, then you *cannot* be partial. So if it is considered wrong for women to speak, then are you not in fault since women should not be doing anything else but being silent? Are you not being double minded to the scripture? People can argue and say that maybe they are just quiet in the "church" as leaders, but did not the scripture say that we are "the CHURCH or the body of Christ?" This means us as women are leaders in and outside of church which enables us to proclaim the word of God.

This brings back to my remembrance about the story of the woman who was caught in the act of adultery. The law says you must present both the man and the women; however, the people only brought forth the adulteress woman to stone her. This is why Jesus said he who is without sin, let him cast the first stone meaning they were hypocrites because they knew the law but they wanted to make it fit them. The people had to drop their stones because they knew they were in the wrong and out of order; if they wanted to punish her then they needed to be punished too. Jesus stopped them from misquoting and misusing scripture which is why he had to make a stand for what is right. It is time to for us to drop the stones and stop leaning to our own understanding. I am only making a statement because we need to be careful not to teach something that we do not fully understand. These stones of religion cause spiritual abortions to take place in the body of Christ.

Satan is a thief and will send people to come against you and the call of God on your life. Often times these individuals are sent not even aware that the enemy is using them to abort God's call for your life. There are too many spiritual abortions going on in the body of Christ. These occurrences happen because people lack wisdom and knowledge, meaning they have a lack of understanding of someone or something. The bibles says in 2 Timothy 2:15, *"Study to shew thyself approved unto God, a workman that needeth not to be ashamed, rightly dividing the word of truth."* The apostle Paul said it like this *"and I intreat thee also, true yokefellow, help those women which arvelo with me in the gospel, with Clement also, and with other my fellow labourers, whose names are in the book of life"* which is founded in Philippians 4:3 (KJV). When you study this passage of scripture, you will notice these two women were already working with the apostle Paul in the gospel.

The Bible says in Matthew 22: 14 (KJV) *"for many are called, but few are chosen."* Looking back at Mary Magdalene, again, you will see that she was called and chosen for leadership. Even when Mary Magdalene traveled with Jesus, He developed women for the Gospel's sake. Jesus let us see that *all* people are equal in God. He allowed women to travel with Him, serve with Him, and support His ministry.

Question: Is God calling you to step out? – Jesus prepared the way for you back then and even now.

_____

_____

_____

Here are some scriptures that can concur that women and men will be used *"freely"* in the gospel. Notice the bolded areas for a better understanding of the scriptures.

[KJV Joel 2: 28-29 "*[28] And it shall come to pass afterward, that I will pour out my spirit upon all flesh; and your sons and your **daughters** shall prophesy, your old men shall dream dreams, your young men shall see visions: [29] And also upon the servants and upon the **handmaids** in those days will I pour out my spirit."*]

[**KJV Acts 2: 14-18** "*¹⁴ But Peter, standing up with the eleven, lifted up his voice, and said unto them, Ye men of Judaea, and all ye that dwell at Jerusalem, be this known unto you, and hearken to my words: ¹⁵ For these are not drunken, as ye suppose, seeing it is but the third hour of the day. ¹⁶ But this is that which was spoken by the prophet Joel; ¹⁷ And it shall come to pass in the last days, saith God, I will pour out of my Spirit upon all flesh: and your sons and your **daughters** shall prophesy, and your young men shall see visions, and your old men shall dream dreams: ¹⁸ And on my servants and on my **handmaidens** I will pour out in those days of my Spirit; and they shall prophesy:…*"]

In the book of the Acts of the Apostles, women were referenced and played a significant role during this particular period in the Bible. Let us read Romans 16:1-2, "*I commend unto you Phebe our sister, which is a servant of the church which is at Cenchrea: ² That ye receive her in the Lord, as becometh saints, and that ye assist her in whatsoever business she hath need of you: for she hath been a succourer of many, and of myself also.*" For example, it was highlighted in the book of Acts that Mary, the mother of Jesus, and other women was there praying with supplications unto the Lord and being on one-accord. They all received the same word to *go* and *wait* until they received power from on high. Through their act of obedience to the word Jesus gave, before ascending unto

Heaven, all of them were empowered with tongues and prophecy- yes women were given the gift! There were men and women there in attendance.

The gift of prophecy was given to both men and women. Let us look at what the bible says in Acts 21:8-9, "*⁸And the next day we that were of Paul's company departed, and came unto Caesarea: and we entered into the house of Philip the evangelist, which was one of the seven; and abode with him. ⁹And the same man had four **daughters**, virgins, which did prophesy.*" According to the scriptures, God used all of Phillips four daughters in the realm of the prophetic. Therefore, if God chooses to use someone's entire family, then it is His doing and will. We must learn to respect who God calls regardless if it's a man or a woman!

God also called women into the office of the Prophet; which they are referred to as a Prophetess. For instance, Miriam was a prophetess who was in the Old Testament.

[**KJV** Exodus 15:20-21 "*²⁰And Miriam the **prophetess**, the sister of Aaron, took a timbrel in her hand; and all the **women** went out after her with timbrels and with dances. ²¹ And Miriam answered them, Sing ye to the*

Lord, for he hath triumphed gloriously; the horse and his rider hath he thrown into the sea."]

Miriam is the sister of Moses and Aaron. She was called into the office of the prophet. As a prophetess, she led the women in dancing and celebrating God's victory over Pharaoh. One thing you can also notice in this scripture was that women went out with her. Women were active and followed even in the Old Testament.

God called Deborah into the office of the prophet as well. Again, another woman that is founded in the Old Testament.

[**KJV Judges 4:4** *"And Deborah, a prophetess, the wife of Lapidoth, she judged Israel at that time."*]

Not only was she used in leadership as a prophetess, but she was selected as a Judge over Israel. Being a judge means that you have a strong voice in government and society. People followed the commands of a judge, but this judge was a woman. She wasn't just a woman, but a wise woman, an encourager, and she also led the people into battle. God chose Deborah for the job and she stepped out in an act of obedience to God's command. Her life teaches us that we need to always be available and be willing to be led by God. This is why the prophet Joel said *"²⁸And it shall come to pass afterward, that I will pour out my spirit upon all flesh; and your sons and your daughters shall prophesy, your old men shall dream dreams, your young men shall see visions: ²⁹And also upon the servants and upon the handmaids in those days will I pour out my spirit"* in Joel 2:28-29 (KJV). The Apostle Peter quoted these same words on the day of Pentecost that he would pour his spirit out upon **all flesh** which includes females.

[**KJV Act 2:16-18** *"¹⁶But this is that which was spoken by the prophet Joel; ¹⁷And it shall come to pass in the last days, saith God, I will pour out of my Spirit upon all flesh: and your sons and your daughters shall prophesy, and your young men shall see visions, and your old men shall dream dreams: ¹⁸And on my servants and on my handmaidens I will pour out in those days of my Spirit; and they shall prophesy:"*]

God used women in many ways to display signs and wonders to show forth His glory. Look at the following scripture about Elizabeth.

[**KJV Luke 1: 36** *"And, behold, thy cousin Elisabeth, she hath also conceived a son in her old age: and this is the sixth month with her, who was called barren."*]

Elizabeth was the wife of Zechariah and the mother of John the Baptist, according to the Gospel of Luke. She had a great call on her life to birth a great gift into the body of Christ; that gift's name was John the Baptist. John the Baptist was a man who God used in a way that many look at his life as an example. He stood apart from the crowd; this was the will of God that John the Baptist stayed away from religion so that he would not be contaminated by it. He was a Nazarene from birth and was filled with the Holy Spirit while in his mother's womb.

Elizabeth's birth was precious and anointed by the Holy Spirit. Even before she gave birth, God used this woman in a special way. Although Elizabeth and Zechariah followed all the Lord's commands, they were both too old to have children. Even though they were too old to have children, God showed Himself to be faithful. You do not have to be a pastor or a preacher for God to use you. God is looking for a vessel that He can show Himself strong and mighty in.

[**KJV 2 Chronicles 16:9** *"For the eyes of the Lord run to and fro throughout the whole earth, to shew himself strong in the behalf of them whose heart is perfect toward him. Herein thou hast done foolishly: therefore from henceforth thou shalt have wars."*]

If anyone questions you about who the power of the Holy Spirit is for, be sure you tell them it is for ALL believers! In church, I heard an awesome woman of God teach a lesson about Priscilla. This lesson really inspired me, as a woman of God, to continue to get to stepping. As I close this chapter, let us look at the lesson she taught:

[**AMP Acts 18:1-3** *AFTER THIS [Paul] departed from Athens and went to Corinth. There he met a Jew named Aquila, a native of Pontus, recently arrived from Italy with Priscilla his wife, due to the fact that Claudius had issued an edict that all the Jews were to leave Rome. And [Paul] went to see them, And because he was of the same occupation, he stayed with them; and they worked [together], for they were tentmakers by trade.*]

We as women should be all that we can be in our homes as well as the ministry. Priscilla was an excellent example that can teach us how to be capable of fulfilling the rightful role as women in and out of the natural and spiritual home. Priscilla shows us about 5 pointers we can apply to be successful in our personal lives as well as ministry. Priscilla shows us as women to get to stepping with determination.

Let's look a little deeper in the scripture of Acts 18 in between verses 1-3 and it states, *"There he met a Jew named Aquila, a native of Pontus, recently arrived from Italy with Priscilla his wife."* This scripture tell us that Aquila was not referenced alone, but his wife Priscilla was referenced along with him. Now throughout the bible, you rarely find a woman being introduced and referenced with her husband. For her to be referenced in such a manner, this must have meant she was an influential person. Being recognized, allowed me to realize that Priscilla stood beside her husband even when they had moved from Rome, she was still there with her husband, Aquila.

Her first point that she shows us as women is her level of dependability for her spouse. Even when it was time to move, she moved with her husband. She did not let him do it alone, but she supported him whole heartedly.

The second point allows us to know that we, as women, can WORK in every aspect both physically and spiritually. Priscilla showed us that she was not a lazy woman, but rather was a hard-working woman. Priscilla and her husband were tentmakers, together, and it was noted they were business owners as well. *"And [Paul] went to see them, And because he was of the same occupation, he stayed with them; and they worked [together], for they were tentmakers by trade."* Priscilla shows us women that she was dedicated to working together as *one* with her husband.

Another point shows us her trust and faithfulness she had in her marriage. As women, we must be trustworthy and faithful to our husbands because it is symbolic to our relationship with God. If you are a single woman, your trust and faithfulness to your spiritual leaders, is equivalent. Aquila trusted his wife. Honestly, what other man do you know would trust another man to live with him and his wife knowing that this man has dealt with a perverse spirit in his past? You must remember that Paul referred to himself as "the chief of all sinners," and which wrote multiple times in the New Testament that everyone should refrain from such sin, sexual immorality, because it is a natural and spirit killer. The perverse spirit is a very strong manipulative and deceiving spirit. Priscilla remained faithful not only to her husband, but her call in ministry alongside with her husband.

Girl, Get to Stepping!

> [**AMP Acts 18:18** *Afterward Paul remained many days longer, and then told the brethren farewell and sailed for Syria; and he was accompanied by Priscilla and Aquila. At Cenchreae he [Paul] cut his hair, for he had made a vow.*]

In this particular passage of scripture, you will see that Priscilla is mentioned before Aquila. This let me know that Paul respected and honored Priscilla not only as the woman of the house, but as a woman in ministry. When Paul departed he left them, Aquila and Priscilla, a charge to continue in ministry together. The charge was to continue the *job* as the Apostles, by leaving them as the Pastors and Apostles of an infant church of the Corinth. Priscilla now has a role as an Apostle and work in ministry as a woman. This means women can take charge in leadership in the church. Priscilla is telling us women that we can lead sheep, if we first knew how to follow.

> [**AMP 1 Corinthians 16:19** *"The churches of Asia send greetings and best wishes. Aquila and Prisca, together with the church [that meets] in their house, send you their hearty greetings in the Lord.*]

Aquila and Priscilla were in ministry together and hosted the church services in their house. Being in ministry together and hosting services in their house shows their commit to the call. How many of you would open up your house for spirits to be left there?

The fourth point that Priscilla shows us as women, is that she accepted the call in ministry. Naturally, she had already shown herself to be a hard-working woman because she used her trade in tent-making; her dependability, trust, and faithfulness to her husband showed that she can fulfill the ministry task that was bestowed upon her from the Apostle Paul. Women, you must get to stepping to the next realm in ministry. You must accept the call to ministry and work in ministry. Don't be afraid of what men may say, but be afraid of what God will do if your disobedience. The bible simply says in Galatians 1:10, *"For do I now persuade men, or God? Or do I seek to please men? For if I yet pleased men, I should not be the servant of Christ."* This is directed not only to the men of God, but also the women of God. We as woman must answer to the call to please God, not please man on their false opinions."

The last point from Priscilla; she had the work of ministry, evangelism, and a strong heart to push the vision of the ministry.

Girl, Get to Stepping!

[**AMP Acts 18:26** *"He began to speak freely (fearlessly and boldly) in the synagogue; but when Priscilla and Aquila heard him, they took him with them and expounded to him the way of God more definitely and accurately.*]

Again, we see that Priscilla's name is mentioned first. Sometimes we, as women, push the vision first before the men because we understand the mission along with the vision because we are the eyes of the ministry. She had a mission. She took her tent-making skills, and built upon it to develop skills to win souls. She did not lose her trade, but she updated it. She was once before making natural houses, but now she was building spiritual houses. She worked with her husband in ministry to help build God's kingdom. Priscilla showed us how we should be as wives. Walking as one with our spouses in ministry, business, and emotionally. She knew when to take lead when her husband might have fallen short. She never stepped outside her lane, but she always worked harmoniously together as a team.

In the body of Christ, we as women need to be Priscilla's. We need to stand up and be dependable, hardworking, faithful, working in leadership, and pushing the vision as women. Priscilla was an active woman in the bible who helped birth the church of Corinth. We must get to stepping in the body of Christ so that we can become impregnated with churches in the spiritual realm. Ministry starts at home, before it takes place in the pulpit. Humble yourself, and work together. The church is in need of Priscilla's. Paraphrasing the scripture of Proverbs 21:19 about a nagging and complaining woman; nobody can't stand a woman who complains and nags, but rather works and fixes the issues.

She accepted the job as an Apostle over a Corinth church, but we know that they told the women to be quiet in the Corinth church because they did not know how to be a Priscilla. They were known as nagging woman who could not be dependable, but just full of words instead of work. They were lazy, loud, unfaithful, and comfortable. They could not humble themselves to the men and work together as one. Paul chose Priscilla to set the example in church today so that women you can get to stepping!

Chapter 3:
Moving Beyond Your Past

[**KJV Jeremiah 29: 11** *"For I know the thoughts that I think toward you, saith the Lord, thoughts of peace, and not of evil, to give you an expected end."*]

God knows our future and knows our plans. There is nothing hidden from Him that He is not already aware of because He is omniscient. We must *never* allow our past to hold us back. If you are dealing with issues, remember God knows all about them. Look at Mary Magdalene; she had many issues going on. Often times Mary Magdalene was identified by her issues. She had seven demons and a spirit of infirmity. Jesus even knew the Samaritan woman at the well had many issues. She had a history of five husbands and the current man she was with was not her spouse. I personally believe these two women may have felt like castaways because others looked down upon them.

Sometimes, I believe people forget they have a past, and have also dealt with a spirit of infirmity by battling with many issues in their lives. Everyone should be and needs to be thankful that God extended His love to us all!

[**KJV Romans 5:8** *"But God commendeth his love toward us, in that, while we were yet sinners, Christ died for us."*]

While we were yet sinners, Christ chose to die for us; this demonstration of His love is truly amazing! Let no one condemn you concerning who God is calling you to become. As people of God, both men and women, you must be confident in who you are even if no one else believes you or believes in you. Always remember God believes in you, which is why he chose "you." There is a gift lying dormant in you waiting to be birthed! Mary Magdalene had a gift in her too, but she needed someone to believe in her… that special someone was Jesus. Not only did Jesus believe in her, but He forgave her and He made her whole.

As I have stated earlier, Mary Magdalene had seven demons cast out of her, and some even say or think she had a bad reputation. The truth is we all have a reputation one way or another. When she came to Jesus, she was cleaned up and was made whole. She was referenced in the four Gospels (Matthew, Mark, Luke, and John) and she was mentioned at least 12 times, which is more than some of the Apostles. Jesus even used her to lead a group of women while they followed Jesus. Jesus equipped this mighty warrior to break generational curses, religion, and tradition. Mary Magdalene was delivered! Christ Jesus had set her free and she was free indeed. She was set free from being bound with seven demons and from her sin. She was thankful for all Jesus had done for her which prompted her to make a choice to become a slave to righteousness. Mary Magdalene was a follower of Jesus Christ and she was His disciple.

> [**KJV Romans 6:18** *"Being then made free from sin, ye became the servants of righteousness."*]
>
> [**KJV Luke 19:10** *"For the Son of man is come to seek and to save that which was lost."*]

Jesus will seek you out; He does not care about your background because He wants to bring you back into the kingdom. He doesn't care about misdemeanors and felonies in the natural or spiritual realm, but more or less your heart. Jesus is not worrying about the things you have done, but is concerned about who you will become. Just like the woman at the well, Jesus had her on His mind. He knew where she was and knew He needed to go through Samaria because there was a divine appointment set. Let us take a look at the word of God:

Girl, Get to Stepping!

[**KJV John 4:6-7** *"⁶ Now Jacob's well was there. Jesus therefore, being wearied with his journey, sat thus on the well: and it was about the sixth hour. ⁷ There cometh a woman of Samaria to draw water: Jesus saith unto her, Give me to drink."*]

As you can see in the text she was on Jesus' mind. The Samaritans were a hated mixed race. Jewish men would not dare to be seen talking to a woman like this under no circumstances; however, Jesus had a plan and a purpose for her. Jesus met her at her low place and knew her faults, but He also knew her need. This woman would soon step into her purpose.

[**KJV John 4: 8-15** *"⁸ (For his disciples were gone away unto the city to buy meat.) ⁹ Then saith the woman of Samaria unto him, How is it that thou, being a Jew, askest drink of me, which am a woman of Samaria? For the Jews have no dealings with the Samaritans. ¹⁰ Jesus answered and said unto her, If thou knewest the gift of God, and who it is that saith to thee, Give me to drink; thou wouldest have asked of him, and he would have given thee living water. ¹¹ The woman saith unto him, Sir, thou hast nothing to draw with, and the well is deep: from whence then hast thou that living water? ¹² Art thou greater than our father Jacob, which gave us the well, and drank thereof himself, and his children, and his cattle? ¹³ Jesus answered and said unto her, Whosoever drinketh of this water shall thirst again: ¹⁴ But whosoever drinketh of the water that I shall give him* *shall n ever thirst; but the water that I shall give him shall be in him a well of water springing up into everlasting life. ^{15} The woman saith unto him, Sir, give me this water, that I thirst not, neither come hither to draw."*]

At this point, according to the passages of scriptures above, we can see that the Samaritan woman's confession had given birth. Everything Jesus talked to her about started to become clear to her. Jesus had to let her see her wrong-doing. The Samaritan woman needed the living water, which is why she asked Jesus for it (refer to verse 15). He was willing to give it to her, but He had to deal with her issues first (refer to verse 16). This meeting with Jesus changed her very foundation. Jesus was *very* patient with her; this is why she asked so many questions although she was receptive and accepted Jesus.

[**KJV John 4: 28-30** *"^{28} The woman then left her waterpot, and went her way into the city, and saith to the men, ^{29} Come, see a man, which told me all things that ever I did: is not this the Christ? ^{30} Then they went out of the city, and came unto him."*]

Let us look at verse 39 of John 4, *"And many of the Samaritans of that city believed on him for the saying of the woman, which testified, He told me all that ever I did."* So girl I say to you **"GIRL, GET TO STEPPING!"**

It is time to stop looking at your past, looking at what you have done, or what others may think of you because they know about you or things you have done. We serve a God that forgives us and does not hold things against us. I am so happy He looks beyond our faults; He does not look at us like man. God will give you beauty for ashes, the oil of joy for mourning, and the garment of praise for the spirit of heaviness. We must understand that we are precious to our heavenly Father; we are the apple of his eye. We are our heavenly Father's masterpiece because we have been created in Christ Jesus.

[KJV Ephesians 2:10 *"For we are his workmanship, created in Christ Jesus unto good works, which God hath before ordained that we should walk in them."*]

Everyone that is in the Bible, every great man and woman, came from a past. The same God then is the same God now.

[KJV Hebrews 13:8 *"Jesus Christ the same yesterday, and today, and forever"*]

He gave them a new heart, He cleaned them with his Holy Spirit, and then placed His Holy Spirit within them to help them and empower them. Do not count yourselves short because you are valuable to the kingdom of God. Girl, get to stepping. You are more than a conqueror, you are the head and not the tail, you are above and not beneath, you can do all things through Christ which strengthens you, you are an overcomer, and you are not a victim… you are victorious! You have a place in the kingdom to workout God's kingdom power here on Earth.

Here are some scriptures to learn, keep, remember, and help you get to stepping while operating in the power of Holy Spirit:

- **<u>God will give us beauty for ashes-</u>**

[**KJV Isaiah 61:3** *"To appoint unto them that mourn in Zion, to give unto them beauty for ashes, the oil of joy for mourning, the garment of praise for the spirit of heaviness; that they might be called trees of righteousness, the planting of the Lord, that he might be glorified."*]

- **We are the head and not the tail-**

[**KJV Deuteronomy 28:13** *"And the Lord shall make thee the head, and not the tail; and thou shalt be above only, and thou shalt not be beneath; if that thou hearken unto the commandments of the Lord thy God, which I command thee this day, to observe and to do them..."*]

- **With God we will always triumph-**

[**KJV Romans 8:31** *"What shall we then say to these things? If God be for us, who can be against us?"*]

- **We are fearfully and wonderfully made-**

[**KJV Psalms 139:14** *"I will praise thee; for I am fearfully and wonderfully made: marvelous are thy works; and that my soul knoweth right well."*]

- **The Champion dwells in you-**

[**KJV 1 John 4:4** *"Ye are of God, little children, and have overcome them: because greater is he that is in you, than he that is in the world."*]

- **We are the apple of His eye-**

[**KJV Zechariah 2:8** *"For thus saith the Lord of hosts; After the glory hath he sent me unto the nations which spoiled you: for he that toucheth you toucheth the apple of his eye."*]

- **There is a river in your belly-**

[**KJV John 7:38** *"He that believeth on me, as the scripture hath said, out of his belly shall flow rivers of living water."*]

There is a river of water that is living in our hearts. As we believe and keep God's Holy Scripture sacred, we will experience our lives being refreshed with healing, deliverance, peace, joy, and love.

Closing:
Girl, Get to Stepping!

[**KJV Joshua 1:9** *"Have not I commanded thee? Be strong and of a good courage; be not afraid, neither be thou dismayed: for the Lord thy God is with thee whithersoever thou goest.*]

The word of God charges us to be strong and courageous in your faith. We must be strong in the Lord and in the power of His might.

[**KJV Ephesians 6:10** *"Finally, my brethren, be strong in the Lord, and in the power of his might."*]

The meaning of courageous in not deterred by danger or pain, but at all times you must be brave. We have to be strong against every fiery dart of the enemy; against darts of deception, religion, and lies.

[**KJV Ephesians 6:12** *"For we wrestle not against flesh and blood, but against principalities, against powers, against the rulers of the darkness of this world, against spiritual wickedness in high places."*]

Warrior women it is time to get to stepping and put on the whole armor of God, which has been made available to every believer. It is important to put on every piece of armor.

Girl, Get to Stepping!

[**KJV Ephesians 6:13-14** *" Wherefore take unto you the whole armour of God, that ye may be able to withstand in the evil day, and having done all, to stand. Stand therefore, having your loins girt about with truth, and having on the breastplate of righteousness."*]

1.) **<u>Loins girded with truth</u>**- Having your loins girded about with truth means you shall know the truth and truth shall make you free.

2.) **<u>The breastplate of righteousness</u>**- Putting on the breastplate of righteousness is living out the truth of God. The breastplate of righteousness is mentioned in the word of God to remind us that we are soldiers in a war against good versus evil. The Apostle Paul warned us that we are in spiritual warfare, and we are going to need every piece of the armor of God in this battle.

3.) **<u>The feet shod with the preparation of the gospel</u>**-

[**KJV Ephesians 6:15** *"And your feet shod with the preparation of the gospel of peace."*]

> [**KJV Romans 10:15** *"And how shall they preach, except they be sent? As it is written, How beautiful are the feet of them that preach the gospel of peace, and bring glad tidings of good things!"*]

> [**KJV Isaiah 52:7** *"How beautiful upon the mountains are the feet of him that bringeth good tidings, that publisheth peace; that bringeth good tidings of good, that publisheth salvation; that saith unto Zion, Thy God reigneth!"*]

When the enemy attacks, you have to remind him that you are the righteousness of God and your steps have been ordered by the Lord.

> [**KJV Psalms 37:23** *"The steps of a good man are ordered by the Lord: and he delighteth in his way."*]

4.) **The shield of faith**- With the shield of faith, the apostle Paul said we shall be able to quench all the fiery darts of the wicked. Faith is a very important piece of armor. This piece of armor helps shield you from the darts of the enemy; that is why it is important that we must have faith!

> [**KJV Hebrews 11:6** *"But without faith it is impossible to please him: for he that cometh to God must believe that he is, and that he is a rewarder of them that diligently seek him."*]

The Bible teaches us that with faith we can speak to mountains.

5.) **<u>The helmet of salvation</u>**- This piece of the armor helps to protect the head (the mind). It helps protect the mind so we can have the mind of Christ.

6.) **<u>The sword of the spirit</u>**- We need to know the word of God and know how to use it. Most importantly, the word of God is a weapon of power and a promise of a sure victory…The apostle Paul decreed and declared that we have been charged to put on the armor of God because it has been made available just for us, but you have to be the one to put it on.

Girl, there is a calling and a dream in you but you have to give birth to it. There are people waiting on you that only you can reach. Step out, it is your time to shine! Step out of anything that is holding you back. You are not a victim, but you are victorious because you are an overcomer. There is an assignment that only you can fulfill. Let fear go! There is a well of power that needs to be released from inside of you. There is a river of God's glory within you. Do not let that dream or vision die, so rise and shine. **"GIRL, GET TO STEPPING!"**

[**KJV Matthew 5:14-16** "*¹⁴ Ye are the light of the world. A city that is set on an hill cannot be hid. ¹⁵ Neither do men light a candle, and put it under a bushel, but on a candlestick; and it giveth light unto all that are in the house. ¹⁶ Let your light so shine before men, that they may see your good works, and glorify your Father which is in heaven."*]

God has called you to be a reflection of Him and not be hidden under a bushel. You shall not to be hidden behind fear, pain, or unforgiveness of your past. You cannot be afraid of what man says vs. what God has said. You are to be a candlestick and shall let the world see the light of God shine through you so the world can see your good works and glorify your heavenly Father. God wants to use you as an example to show the world that whom the Son sets free is truly free indeed! Romans 8:30 says *"Moreover whom he did predestinate, them he also called: and whom he called, them he also justified: and whom he justified, them he also glorified* (KJV)." It is important that we deny ourselves and go after the things in the kingdom of God.

[**KJV Luke 9:23** *"And he said to them all, If any man will come after me, let him deny himself, and take up his cross daily, and follow me."*]

Let us take up our cross and follow Jesus. You have been given the right not to remain or be silent but to follow after Jesus Christ! Isaiah 58:1 said it best *"Cry aloud, spare not, lift up thy voice like a trumpet, and shew my people their transgression, and the house of Jacob their sins* (KJV)." Hell needs to hear the authority that Jesus has given to you! Victory is all over you, so again I say… **"GIRL, GET TO STEPPING!"**

[**KJV Matthew 5:17** *"Think not that I am come to destroy the law, or the prophets: I am not come to destroy, but to fulfil."*]

In the passage of scripture referenced above, when Jesus said that he did not come to do away with the law or the prophets… He meant the will of His Father is to bring understanding and truth. Jesus knew there would be some people that would misunderstand the law and the prophets, which is the same way in today's time that we live in. Many today read the Holy Bible but misunderstand the scriptures.

[**KJV 2 Timothy 2:15** *"Study to shew thyself approved unto God, a workman that needeth not to be ashamed, rightly dividing the word of truth."*]

We must refrain from not dividing the word of truth rightly.

[**KJV James 1:5** *"If any of you lack wisdom, let him ask of God, that giveth to all men liberally, and upbraideth not; and it shall be given him."*]

If you do not understand something, you must go in prayer and tell God, in faith, that you lack understanding before just saying or teaching something incorrectly. In faith, you need to ask the Holy Spirit to teach you.

[**KJV Proverbs 4:7** *"Wisdom is the principal thing; therefore get wisdom: and with all thy getting get understanding."*]

Remember, God has your back; He just needs you to get stepping. Do not let fear of your family and/or friends stop you from obeying God. Girl, get to stepping out of that pit you are in. God's plan for you is much greater than where you are right now.

[**KJV 1 Corinthians 2:9** *"But as it is written, Eye hath not seen, nor ear heard, neither have entered into the heart of man, the things which God hath prepared for them that love him."*]

In my closing, I would like for you to make this declaration with me:

Girl, get to stepping,

Step out of your past,

Step out of your mess,

Step out of your disappointment,

Step out of worrying about what other people may think or say about you,

Step out of being unsure of yourself

Step out of fear,

Step out of bondage,

Step out of religion,

Step out of tradition,

Step out of self,

GIRL, GET TO STEPPING!

Apostle/Prophetess Ann Harris

Epilogue

[**KJV 1 Corinthians 2:9** *"But as it is written, Eye hath not seen, nor ear heard, neither have entered into the heart of man, the things which God hath prepared for them that love him."*]

[**KJV Colossians 1:13** *"Who hath delivered us from the power of darkness, and hath translated us into the kingdom of his dear Son."*]

We are God's vessels. We have been chosen to be a part of God's plan to reach the world and to be a witness of His love and forgiving power. When we receive Jesus Christ as Lord over our lives, the Holy Spirit comes into our hearts. After this has taken place, a new work can begin. The Holy Spirit will guide us into all truths and will show us things to come, but we have to let Him.

[**KJV John 15:16** *"Ye have not chosen me, but I have chosen you, and ordained you, that ye should go and bring forth fruit, and that your fruit should remain: that whatsoever ye shall ask of the Father in my name, he may give it you."*]

Jesus chose us to go and to be fruitful; therefore, we are not to limit ourselves but instead we should bear fruit. Jesus said He will give us strength to love, to forgive, and to carry out his mission. The Holy Spirit will teach, encourage you, and will help you become everything that you need to become. You have to accept that there is more to this *walk* than just saying you are *saved* and that you go to church. There is greater in you. There is a power in you, so are you willing to accept or reject His offer?

I encourage you to go and bear fruit. There is a testimony in you. Do not let fear or religion control you. Religion is a form of being in prison and fear is like being in charge over it. When I was in the world, no one could control me or tell me what I could and could not do because I did whatever it took to prove my point, which was to make them out of a lie. The point I am making is this, now that you and I are in Christ Jesus, we have to get the same mentality when it comes down to religion and fear. The apostle James said it like this *"Ye adulterers and adulteresses, know ye not that the friendship of the world is enmity with God? Whosoever therefore will be a friend of the world is the enemy of God* (KJV James 4:4)." I have decided that now that I am a new creature in God, I will not give the world more than I will give God because he brought me out of darkness.

[**KJV 2 Corinthians 5:17** *"Therefore if any man be in Christ, he is a new creature: old things are passed away; behold, all things are become new."*]

[**KJV 1 Peter 2:9** *"But ye are a chosen generation, a royal priesthood, an holy nation, a peculiar people; that ye should shew forth the praises of him who hath called you out of darkness into his marvelous light."*]

[**KJV Philippians 1:6** *"Being confident of this very thing, that he which hath begun a good work in you will perform it until the day of Jesus Christ."*]

We must be confident in the One that called us and we must be confident in what God said about us. His word declares that we are more than conquerors and that if God be for us then who can be against us. God has begun a good work in us. He has given us His Holy Spirit, His word, and His promise. There is a work that He wants to perform in you, but He longs for your obedience and your "yes" as a sign of total that you totally surrender, and you will allow Him to use you how He sees fit.

[**KJV Mark 16:17-18** *"17 And these signs shall follow them that believe; In my name shall they cast out devils; they shall speak with new tongues; 18 They shall take up serpents; and if they drink any deadly thing, it shall not hurt them; they shall lay hands on the sick, and they shall recover."*]

We must keep in mind that one of the greatest tactics of the enemy is the spirit of religion. Religion is a controlling spirit that wants to strip you of your power and authority. So women of God, let us remember it is time to fight back and break these chains of religion off our lives. Whom the Son sets free is truly free indeed, so I say to you, "***Girl, Get to Stepping!***"

Prayer

I pray that I rise and shine. I pray that I step out of everything that may be holding me back from obeying God's call for my life. I pray that the power of fear and religion has to be broken off of me and that I will walk in the power of an overcomer because victory belongs to me. I know that I am more than a conqueror; greater works shall I do. God has given me power to tread on scorpions and serpents. I take authority over my life today. I speak life over me and every gift and every assignment that is in me; it shall live and not die. I am a mighty warrior woman. I pray that a fresh anointing will rest upon me and that every prison door that held me hostage will no longer keep me bound. I give God praise for no weapon that is formed against me shall not prosper. I praise Jesus and I give Him all the honor and glory in Jesus name, Amen.

Apostle/Prophetess Ann Harris

Questions for You

1- Do you believe that God called you?
_____
_____
_____
_____
_____

2- How do you see yourself in the ministry?
_____
_____
_____
_____
_____

Girl, Get to Stepping!

3- Are you a person that is easy to be offended? *(Do you get in your feelings quickly?)*

_____
_____
_____
_____
_____
_____

4- Are you a person that has let fear keep you in bondage? How?

_____
_____
_____
_____
_____
_____

5- Have you made up your mind to overcome religious beliefs based on man's doctrine?

_____
_____
_____
_____
_____

Seeking the Lord Scriptures

1 Chronicles 22:19

Now set your heart and your soul to seek the Lord your God; arise therefore, and build ye the sanctuary of the Lord God, to bring the ark of the covenant of the Lord, and the holy vessels of God, into the house that is to be built to the name of the Lord.

Psalms 14:2

The Lord looked down from heaven upon the children of men, to see if there were any that did understand, and seek God.

1 Chronicles 16:11

Seek the Lord and his strength, seek his face continually.

Hosea 10:12

Sow to yourselves in righteousness, reap in mercy; break up your fallow ground: for it is time to seek the Lord, till he come and rain righteousness upon you.

Proverbs 8:17

I love them that love me; and those that seek me early shall find me.

Zephaniah 2:3

Seek ye the Lord, all ye meek of the earth, which have wrought his judgment; seek righteousness, seek meekness: it may be ye shall be hid in the day of the Lord's anger.

Deuteronomy 4:29-31

But if from thence thou shalt seek the Lord thy God, thou shalt find him, if thou seek him with all thy heart and with all thy soul. When thou art in tribulation, and all these things are come upon thee, even in the latter days, if thou turn to the Lord thy God, and shalt be obedient unto his voice; (For the Lord thy God is a merciful God;) he will not forsake thee, neither destroy thee, nor forget the covenant of thy fathers which he sware unto them.

Matthew 7:7-8

Ask, and it shall be given you; seek, and ye shall find; knock, and it shall be opened unto you: For every one that asketh receiveth; and he that seeketh findeth; and to him that knocketh it shall be opened.

Psalms 27:8

When thou saidst, Seek ye my face; my heart said unto thee, Thy face, Lord, will I seek.

Jeremiah 29:13

And ye shall seek me, and find me, when ye shall search for me with all your heart.

Matthew 6:33

But seek ye first the kingdom of God, and his righteousness; and all these things shall be added unto you.

Psalms 27:4

One thing have I desired of the Lord, that will I seek after; that I may dwell in the house of the Lord all the days of my life, to behold the beauty of the Lord, and to enquire in his temple.

Matthew 13:44-46

Again, the kingdom of heaven is like unto treasure hid in a field; the which when a man hath found, he hideth, and for joy thereof goeth and selleth all that he hath, and buyeth that field. Again, the kingdom of heaven is like unto a merchant man, seeking goodly pearls: Who, when he had found one pearl of great price, went and sold all that he had, and bought it.

Psalms 119:2

Blessed are they that keep his testimonies and that seek him with the whole heart.

Apostle/Prophetess Ann Harris

Jeremiah 33:3
Call unto me, and I will answer thee, and show thee great and mighty things, which thou knowest not.

1 Peter 5:7
Casting all your care upon him; for he careth for you.

Isaiah 26:3
Thou wilt keep him in perfect peace, whose mind is stayed on thee: because he trusteth in thee.

Psalms 120:1
In my distress I cried unto the Lord, and he heard me.

Speaking Life and Overcoming Scriptures

Psalms 27:1

The Lord is my light and my salvation; whom shall I fear? the Lord is the strength of my life; of whom shall I be afraid?

Psalms 55:22

Cast thy burden upon the LORD, and he shall sustain thee: he shall never suffer the righteous to be moved.

Isaiah 41:13

For I the Lord thy God will hold thy right hand, saying unto thee, Fear not; I will help thee.

James 1:19-21

Wherefore, my beloved brethren, let every man be swift to hear, slow to speak, slow to wrath: For the wrath of man worketh not the righteousness of God. Wherefore lay apart all filthiness and superfluity of naughtiness, and receive with meekness the engrafted word, which is able to save your souls.

1 Peter 5:7

Casting all your care upon him; for he careth for you.

Psalms 31:24

Be of good courage, and he shall strengthen your heart, all ye that hope in the Lord.

Philippians 4:13

I can do all things through Christ which strengtheneth me.

Isaiah 41:10

Fear thou not; for I am with thee: be not dismayed; for I am thy God: I will strengthen thee; yea, I will help thee; yea, I will uphold thee with the right hand of my righteousness.

James 1:2-4

My brethren, count it all joy when ye fall into divers temptations; Knowing this, that the trying of your faith worketh patience. But let patience have her perfect work, that ye may be perfect and entire, wanting nothing.

Romans 8:28

And we know that all things work together for good to them that love God, to them who are the called according to his purpose.

John 14:27

Peace I leave with you, my peace I give unto you: not as the world giveth, give I unto you. Let not your heart be troubled, neither let it be afraid.

Scriptures for Help

Romans 12:1-2

I beseech you therefore, brethren, by the mercies of God, that ye present your bodies a living sacrifice, holy, acceptable unto God, which is your reasonable service. And be not conformed to this world: but be ye transformed by the renewing of your mind, that ye may prove what is that good, and acceptable, and perfect, will of God.

Psalms 51:10

Create in me a clean heart, O God; and renew a right spirit within me.

Colossians 3:15

And let the peace of God rule in your hearts, to the which also ye are called in one body; and be ye thankful.

Philippians 4:7

And the peace of God, which passeth all understanding, shall keep your hearts and minds through Christ Jesus.

Romans 8:30

Moreover whom he did predestinate, them he also called: and whom he called, them he also justified: and whom he justified, them he also glorified.

Psalms 119:16

I will delight myself in thy statutes: I will not forget thy word.

Romans 14:19

Let us therefore follow after the things which make for peace, and things wherewith one may edify another.

Psalms 29:11

The Lord will give strength unto his people; the Lord will bless his people with peace.

Apostle/Prophetess Ann Harris

Personal Notes

Girl, Get to Stepping!

Personal Notes

Apostle/Prophetess Ann Harris

Personal Notes

_____
_____
_____
_____
_____
_____
_____
_____
_____
_____
_____
_____
_____
_____

Girl, Get to Stepping!

Personal Notes

_____
_____
_____
_____
_____
_____
_____
_____
_____
_____
_____
_____
_____
_____
_____
_____

Personal Notes

For More Information:

at **ApostleAnnMinistries**

E-mail: apostleannministries@gmail.com

www.apostleannministries.com

For Booking Information:

E-mail: bookingapostleann@gmail.com

Ordering Information:

Search: Apostle/Prophetess Ann Harris

For more ordering information and locations to purchase, ***"Girl, Get to Stepping!"***
E-mail: apostleannministries@gmail.com

Other Information:

www.dailywalkministries.com

www.ingramcontent.com/pod-product-compliance
Lightning Source LLC
Chambersburg PA
CBHW051710040426
42446CB00008B/812